Emma Garfield

Crock Pot

Recipe book UK

The Best and Easiest Daily Slow Cooker Recipes for Everyday

All rights reserved

ISBN : 9798366331647

Contents

Introduction 6

Stuffed chicken thigh rolls...............................7

Beans with veal shank.......................................8

Pork shoulder with rice......................................9

Sky Bacon..10

Chicken with Green Beans................................11

Pork leg with barbecue sauce.........................13

Sirloin fillet, raw ham and cheese..................14

Pork sirloin in red wine.....................................15

Beans with ribs and tagarninas......................16

Cream Cheese Chicken Breasts.......................17

Chicken with potatoes 18

Chicken hindquarters with tomato................19

pork ribs 20

Curry Apple Sherry 21

Pork tenderloin in red wine 23

Red pepper salad with tuna............................24

Beans with Pork Ribs...25

Round chicken stuffed with ham and cheese..26

Rice with tagarninas and clams......................27

Chickpeas with spinach 28

Melva with red peppers 29

Pork leg with sauce and red peppers 30

Veal rolls 31

Chicken breast with peppers 32

Chickpeas with Swiss chard 33

Veal Broth 34

Pork leg in red wine 35

Rosemary Pork Chops 36

Veal churrascos 37

Chicken thighs 38

Chicken cooked in beer 39

Chicken thighs with beans 40

Chicken steaks with vegetables 41

Chickpea menudo 42

Multi-meat dish 44

Pork head loin 45

Calf at the planter 46

Iberian loin 47

Potatoes with meat, green beans and carrots 48

Iberian pork cheek 50

Chickpeas with Swiss chard 51

Potatoes with Swiss chard 52

Vegetables with eggs 53

Chicken thighs with vegetables 54

Beef with tomato 55

Turkey breast roll 56

Chicken with carrots 57

Beef with vegetables... 58

Chicken breasts 59

Pork loin with bun 60

Pork loin with herbs, thyme and rosemary 61

Veal chop with potatoes and paprika 63

Potatoes with ribs 64

Pork Loin with Worcestershire Sauce 65

Potatoes with beef... 66

Pork meat with Pedro Jiménez 68

Whiskey sirloin 69

Lentils with green beans and carrots... 70

Sausages in wine 71

Roasted peppers with mozzarella balls 72

Chicken with mushrooms and rice.. 73

Loin stuffed with cheddar and ham 74

Cauliflower soup 75

Chicken hindquarter with thyme 76

Beef spaghetti 77

Pork loin with zucchini 78

Beef steak with mushrooms 79

Pork stew with vegetables 80

Introduction

The slow cooker has become one of the most used appliances in the kitchen today. The first model was introduced to us in 1970, marketed strictly as a bean cooker.

Over time, the brand has expanded its cooking repertoire to include many different types of dishes. The company then redesigned its grain cooker by redesigning it and adding handles and a glass lid.

Subsequently, the product was registered under the trade name "Crock-Pot", which is now sold under this brand. Now, of course, the word "slow cooker" has become a generic term used to refer to any type of "Crock-Pot" or "Slow-Cooker".

Types of slow cooker Crock pot

The electronic programmable slow cooker Crock pot

It has electronic controls and a digital timer allowing you to choose the cooking time. Some allow you to program the slow cooker for up to 24 hours in 30 minute increments and the digital display shows the cooking time remaining. All models tested automatically switch to a keep warm setting when the set time is up and can keep food warm for hours. Some also have a manual mode.

The manual slow cooker crock pot

All you have to do is simply turn the control to the desired setting — low, medium or high. Manual models don't have a timer, so you'll need to watch the cooking, especially for small amounts of more delicate foods, and you'll need to turn off the slow cooker. Some models have a keep warm setting, but you will need to switch to this mode.

Stuffed chicken thigh rolls

For 4 people

Ingredients

- 4 chicken thighs
- 4 slices of cheese
- 4 slices of raw ham
- Salt
- Ground pepper
- Extra virgin olive oil
- 1 glass of wine

Instructions

1. We flatten the thighs so that the meat is thinner. We remove the skin if it had any and any bones.
2. We place the slice of cheese and the slice of ham in the center.
3. We ride pressing well.
4. We cross with a toothpick to better hold.
5. In the bowl of the Crock Pot we put a little extra virgin olive oil.
6. We place the four rolls.
7. Season with salt and pepper and add the wine and a little water, like half a glass.
8. Cover the Crock Pot and select High, 3 hours.
9. We serve.

Beans with veal shank

For: 4 people

Ingredients

- 250 g of beans
- 300 g of veal shank
- 1 potato + 1 onion
- 4 garlic cloves
- Extra virgin olive oil
- Salt + Ground pepper
- Thyme + Cumin
- Paprika

Instructions

1. We put the beans to soak for at least 8 hours.
2. Chop the onion and the garlic cloves and put them in a pan with a little extra virgin olive oil.
3. We cook the sauce over low heat until the onion is transparent.
4. Chop the veal shank into cubes and add it to the sauce.
5. We jump.
6. In the bowl of the Crock Pot, we put the drained beans in the water where they were soaked.
7. Peel the potato and cut it into pieces. We place in the bowl of the Crock Pot.
8. We incorporate the sauce and the shank.
9. We blend.
10. We add water, just enough so that the porridge can cook, it does not have to cover everything.
11. We put salt, paprika, thyme and cumin to taste.
12. We remove to mix everything.
13. Select the low temperature in the Crock Pot and cook for 12 hours.
14. We rectify the salt if necessary.
15. We serve.

Pork shoulder with rice

For: 4 people

Ingredients

- 1 pork shoulder
- 1 onion
- 4 garlic cloves
- 1 green pepper
- 1 carrot
- ½ zucchini
- Extra virgin olive oil
- Salt
- Ground pepper
- 1 glass of red wine

Instructions

1. We put a generous amount of extra virgin olive oil in a pan.
2. Season the pork shoulder and brown it in the pan on all sides.
3. Add the wine and bring to a boil.
4. We move on to the Crock Pot bowl.
5. In this same pan we put a little oil and the onion, garlic, pepper, zucchini and carrot, all peeled and chopped.
6. We fry and when it's tender, we go to the Crock Pot.
7. Cover and cook in Alto for about 4 hours.
8. We transfer all the vegetables to a saucepan with the juices and let them reduce over medium heat.
9. We reserve the meat.
10. We cook the rice in water with a little salt.
11. We cut the meat into fillets.
12. The vegetables are crushed when they are well reduced.
13. We serve the meat with the sauce and cooked rice.

Sky Bacon

For 4 people

Ingredients
- 9 egg yolks
- 3 whole eggs
- 250ml water
- 300 g of sugar
- 75 gr of sugar and 40 ml of water for caramel

Instructions
1. The first thing we are going to do is put the mold that we are going to use inside the bucket and add water to only half of the mold. We remove the mold and leave the water inside the Crock Pot. Select High Heat and allow the water to heat up while preparing the rest of the recipe.
2. We make the caramel in a saucepan and put it in the bottom of the mold.
3. We put sugar and water in a saucepan so that the syrup is made. About 15 minutes or so.
4. We beat the yolks and eggs.
5. Add the hot syrup, little by little and without stirring.
6. We put the mixture in the mold, in my case I divided it between the four molds.
7. Cover tightly with aluminum foil.
8. We put the mold in the bowl of the Crock Pot.
9. We leave between 2 to 3 hours, at high temperature. Much will depend on the size of our sky bacon, so we only have to click on the first two hours and when the sky bacon is curdled, we remove it.
10. Unmold when the sky bacon is cold.
11. We serve as is or we can serve with whipped cream, liquid caramel and nuts.

Chicken with Green Beans

For: 4 people

Ingredients

- 1 ground chicken
- Salt
- Ground pepper
- 1 onion
- 4 garlic cloves
- 1 tomato
- 1 green pepper
- Extra virgin olive oil
- 1 glass of wine
- 1 tray of fresh green beans or a jar of green beans

Instructions

1. I like to remove the skin from the chicken when I'm going to cook it so it doesn't leave the stew very greasy, so you remove the skin from the chicken that you've cut into pieces.
2. We put the chicken in the bowl of the Crock Pot.
3. We reserve.
4. In a large pan we put the onion, pepper, garlic and tomato, all very chopped. I like to chop it in the Thermomix 5 seconds, speed 5 and then add the oil and make the sauce with 7 minutes, 120 degrees temperature, speed 1. If we want to make the sauce in the pan, just chop, put the oil and make the sauce over low heat.
5. Add the sofrito to the Crock Pot bowl and stir.
6. Season with salt and pepper.
7. We add the wine and the chopped green beans if they are fresh, if they come from a pot we leave it for when the chicken is cooked.
8. We select in the Crock Pot, high doneness, 4 hours. If the green beans are in a pot, now is the time to drain them, add them, toss and let sit for another 30 minutes.

9. We transfer the chicken to a dish and set aside.
10. All the sauce that has the Crock Pot bucket we put it in a saucepan and take it to the fire to reduce it.
11. We let the sauce reduce until it thickens to our liking.
12. Add the sauce over the chicken.
13. We serve.

Pork leg with barbecue sauce

For 4 people

Ingredients

- 1 piece of pork thigh
- 1 onion
- 1 glass of red wine
- 1 tablespoon of soy sauce
- 3 tablespoons barbecue sauce
- Salt
- Ground pepper
- Extra virgin olive oil

Instructions

1. We put in a frying pan a bottom of extra virgin olive oil.
2. Add the chopped onion and let it fry.
3. When the onion is golden, go to the bowl of the Crock Pot.
4. In the same pan, we now brown the meat on all sides.
5. Season with salt and pepper, add red wine and soy sauce.
6. Bring to a boil and transfer to the Crock Pot everything, the meat and the juices.
7. Add a large glass of water or meat stock.
8. We cover and leave in the high position, 3 or 4 hours, it will depend on the size of the room.
9. We remove the meat and reserve it.
10. We pass to a casserole all the juices with the onion.
11. Add barbecue sauce and mix.
12. We reduced the fire.
13. Crush with the blender.
14. We serve the meat cut into fillets with the sauce on top.

Sirloin fillet, raw ham and cheese

For 4 people

Ingredients

- 1 loaf of bread
- Sirloin slices
- Ham slices
- Slices of cheese

Instructions

1. We open the thread and put a layer of thinly sliced sirloin slices on it.
2. On the sirloin we place the slices of cheese.
3. On the cheese we place the slices of raw ham.
4. We cover the wire and take in the oven.
5. Bake at 170 degrees for about 10 minutes, just enough to warm the bread without burning it, brown the cheese so it melts and the filling inside is warm and rich.
6. We cut and serve immediately.

Pork sirloin in red wine

For 4 people

Ingredients

- 1 pork tenderloin
- 1 onion
- 1 leek
- 1 piece of red pepper
- 4 garlic cloves
- 1 tomato
- Extra virgin olive oil
- Salt
- Ground pepper
- 1 glass of red wine

Instructions

1. Chop the onion, leek, red pepper, garlic and tomato.
2. We put everything in a large pan with a background of extra virgin olive oil.
3. We make the sofrito and when we have the vegetables ready, we pass it into the bowl of the Crock Pot.
4. In the same skillet, brown the sirloin on all sides.
5. Season with salt and pepper and add the wine.
6. We bring to a strong boil and transfer the sirloin to the bowl of the Crock Pot with all the juices from the pan.
7. We put a small glass of hot water or vegetable broth.
8. Cover the Crock Pot and select low heat and cook for 6 hours.
9. We remove the sirloin and cut it as we want to use it.
10. All the vegetables are crushed, but before putting them on the fire to reduce the juice. We grind well and have a great sauce to serve with the meat or store in a jar for future recipes.

Beans with ribs and tagarninas

For 4 people

Ingredients

- 250g cinnamon beans
- 500g pork ribs
- 1 platter of tagarnina
- 1 onion
- 4 garlic cloves
- Extra virgin olive oil
- Salt
- Ground pepper
- Cumin
- Paprika

Instructions

1. We put the beans in plenty of water the night before, or at least 8 hours before we start cooking.
2. Chop the onion and the garlic cloves.
3. We put the onion and garlic in a pan with extra virgin olive oil.
4. When the onion is fried, add the chopped ribs.
5. We fried the ribs.
6. We remove the pan and add the paprika and stir quickly.
7. Wash the tagarninas and drain well.
8. We put the drained beans in the Crock Pot.
9. Add the onion with the ribs and the tagarninas.
10. We cover with water, salons and peppers and add a little cumin.
11. We leave in the Crock Pot, at low temperature, 12 hours.
12. We rectify the salt.
13. We serve.

Cream Cheese Chicken Breasts

For 4 people

Ingredients

- 4 chicken breasts
- 1 onion
- 75 g sliced mushrooms
- 12 mushrooms
- 1 brick of cream, 200 ml
- 40 g of grated cheese
- Extra virgin olive oil
- Salt
- Ground pepper

Instructions

1. Salt and pepper the chicken breasts.
2. Chop the bacon in case it is no longer cut into strips and plasticize the mushrooms.
3. Chop the onion.
4. In a pan we put a little extra virgin olive oil.
5. Add the breasts and brown.
6. We pass them to the Crock Pot.
7. We put the onion in the same pan and let it cook over low heat until the onion is transparent.
8. Then add the mushrooms and bacon.
9. Sauté until the mushrooms are tender.
10. Add the robe and the grated cheese.
11. Mix well and season.
12. Add to Crock Pot, covering chicken breasts well.
13. Cook over low heat for 4 hours, a little more if the breasts are very thick.
14. We serve.

Chicken with potatoes

For 4 people

Ingredients

- 1 chicken
- 4 potatoes
- Salt
- Ground pepper
- garlic powder
- Thyme
- Winemaker Sherry
- Extra virgin olive oil

Instructions

1. We peel the potatoes and cut them into slices.
2. We put the Crock Pot with salt and ground pepper.
3. Add a few threads of oil.
4. In a bowl we put a base of extra virgin olive oil and add salt, ground pepper, garlic powder, thyme and sherry vinegar.
5. Mix well and paint, using a silicone brush, all the chicken. First we paint the part of the back to be able to place the chicken on the potatoes then we paint the whole top of the breasts and thighs.
6. We take the Crock Pot on low and leave 10 am.
7. We remove the chicken, we remove the potatoes and the juice that was in the bucket, we reduce it in a saucepan.
8. Pour over the chicken.
9. We serve.

Chicken hindquarters with tomato

For 4 people

Ingredients

- 4 minced chicken hindquarters
- 1 onion
- 4 garlic cloves
- Salt
- Ground pepper
- 1 large can of crushed tomatoes
- 1 glass of wine
- Optional, a little aromatic herb.

Instructions

1. Chop the onion and the garlic cloves.
2. We put in a casserole a bottom of extra virgin olive oil.
3. When hot, add the onion and garlic cloves.
4. Fry over low heat and when the onion is transparent, add the can of crushed tomato, season with salt and pepper, and when it begins to boil, remove from the heat.
5. We brown the chicken in a pan with a little extra virgin olive oil.
6. When we have all the chicken browned, add the wine and bring to a boil.
7. We pass the chicken in the casserole where we have the sauce and the tomato.
8. We mix and pour everything into the bowl of the Crock Pot.
9. We select high and cook for 3 hours.
10. We serve.

pork ribs

For 4 people

Ingredients

- 1 or 2 strings of ribs
- Salt
- Ground pepper
- Thyme
- garlic powder
- Extra virgin olive oil

Instructions

1. In a small bowl we put a good spray of extra virgin olive oil.
2. Add salt, ground pepper, garlic powder and thyme.
3. We mix well
4. We comb the rib strings on all sides.
5. We put the ribs in the Crock Pot no matter if they are on top of each other.
6. We select 8 o'clock, low temperature position.
7. We pass the ribs on the baking sheet.
8. Pour the juice from the Crock Pot bowl over the ribs
9. Bake at 180 degrees, about 20 minutes or so, turning the ribs to brown on all sides.
10. We serve.

Curry Apple Sherry

For 4 people

Ingredients

- 300 g of chickpeas
- 100 g white beans
- 1 bunch Swiss chard
- 1 bunch of celery
- 1 head of garlic
- Extra virgin olive oil
- 1 slice of bread
- 1 tablespoon sweet pepper
- 1 teaspoon ground cumin
- 4 cloves
- 1 piece of fresh bacon
- 1 piece of double chin bacon
- 1 horseshoe sweet chorizo
- 1 black pudding horseshoe
- 1 piece of loin head, about 1 kilo
- 1 string of pork ribs
- 2 potatoes
- 1 pork trot

Instructions

1. We put the chickpeas and white beans to soak.
2. Drain and add to Crock Pot bowl.
3. We cover with hot water.
4. We put 2 hours up.
5. After 2 hours we put all the pringá, bacon, meat, ribs, pig's feet, chorizo and blood sausage on the legumes. If we have to chop for it to fit better in the Crock Pot, it's done.
6. We cover and let continue cooking in the Alto.
7. We separate the leaves of Swiss chard from the trunks. We reserve the Swiss chard leaves and cut the stems.
8. We cut celery stalks.
9. Peel the potatoes and chop them.
10. We put the three ingredients on the pringá.
11. We put salt.
12. Cover and cook. Between that we prepared the pringá and the vegetables, he cooked another hour, we did three hours.

13. In a pan we put the peeled and whole garlic with a bottom of extra virgin olive oil.
14. Fry and add the slice of bread.
15. We fry the bread and add paprika, cumin and cloves.
16. Quickly remove and remove from heat.
17. We cover with water.
18. Once the bread is well soaked, put everything in the glass of the blender and grind it.
19. Add to slow cooker bowl. We remove well, but moving the bucket, we don't put anything inside that could break the pringá or the legumes.
20. We leave 7 to 8 hours in height, it will depend on the size of the pieces of the pringá.
21. When serving, we carefully pass the pringá to a spring.
22. We serve the vegetables on a plate with the vegetables for a first course and the fats for a second course.

Pork tenderloin in red wine

For 4 people

Ingredients

- 1 large pork tenderloin
- 1 carrot
- 1 onion
- 4 garlic cloves
- 300ml red wine
- 2 or 3 grated tomatoes
- Extra virgin olive oil
- Black pepper
- Salt
- fresh parsley

Instructions

1. Season sirloin with salt and pepper and sprinkle with chopped parsley.
2. We brown the sirloin in a pan with a little extra virgin olive oil. Chop carrots and onion.
3. We grate the tomato. We take out the sirloin and put the Crock Pot.
4. In this same container with a little oil, we put the onion, carrots, peeled and whole garlic.
5. We fry a little and season with salt and pepper.
6. Add the red wine and boil for about 10 minutes.
7. We spent it all in the Crock Pot bucket.
8. We cook for 4 to 6 hours on BAJA. The time will depend on the size of the sirloin. We remove the sirloin to a plate.
9. We crush the vegetables with the blender and if we want it even finer, we can pass it through a Chinese.
10. If we want the sauce to be even denser or thicker, we just have to let it reduce on the fire.
11. We cut the sirloin into medallions and serve it with the sauce.

Red pepper salad with tuna

For 4 people

Ingredients

- 2 or 3 red peppers
- 1 bottle of tuna in oil
- 1 chives
- 2 cloves garlic
- Salt
- Extra virgin olive oil
- Winemaker Sherry

Instructions

1. We paint the peppers with extra virgin olive oil and leave the inside of the Crock Pot.
2. We added a little salt.
3. Cover and leave on high for about 4 hours.
4. We turn off and leave the peppers inside and covered to cool.
5. Peel the peppers, remove the seeds and cut them into strips.
6. We put the peppers in a bowl.
7. Add the two very minced garlic cloves and the chopped chives.
8. We blend.
9. Add salt, extra virgin olive oil and vinegar, to taste.
10. Mix again.
11. We take in the refrigerator at least 1 hour.
12. Drain belly and spread over peppers.
13. We serve.

Beans with Pork Ribs

For 4 people

Ingredients

- 250g cinnamon beans
- 500g pork ribs
- 200 g of green beans
- 1 onion
- 4 garlic cloves
- Extra virgin olive oil
- Salt and ground pepper
- Thyme
- Cumin
- Paprika

Instructions

1. We put the beans in plenty of water for at least 8 hours to hydrate them.
2. Chop the onion and the garlic cloves, fry them in a pan with extra virgin olive oil.
3. When we have the transparent onion, add the chopped ribs to brown them well.
4. When we are going to remove the pan, add the paprika, stir quickly so that it does not burn and turn off the heat.
5. Chop the green beans.
6. We put the drained beans in the Crock Pot with the green beans and the contents of the pot.
7. Cover with water, season with salt and pepper and add a little thyme and cumin.
8. We leave in the Crock Pot, at low temperature, 12 hours.
9. We rectify the salt if necessary.
10. We serve.

Round chicken stuffed with ham and cheese

For 4 people

Ingredients

- 1 piece of chicken stuffed with ham and cheese
- 4-6 shallots
- Extra virgin olive oil
- garlic powder
- 1 glass of wine
- Salt
- Ground pepper
- Nut

Instructions

1. We put the peeled and chopped shallots in the bowl of the Crock Pot.
2. Add a few drizzles of oil and place the round chicken on top.
3. Season with salt and pepper and add the wine.
4. Sprinkle with garlic powder.
5. Cover and cook at low temperature for about 4 hours.
6. We remove the meat and if it has a grill, we remove it. We let it cool .
7. We put the shallots together with the juices in the glass of the blender.
8. We crush.
9. We pass the sauce in a saucepan and set on fire to thicken the sauce.
10. We rectify the salt.
11. Add the peeled walnuts to the sauce.
12. We serve the meat cut into slices with the shallot and walnut sauce.

Rice with tagarninas and clams

For: 4 people

Ingredients

- 1 onion
- 4 garlic cloves
- 1 bag of tagarnina
- 1 stitch of clams
- 1 large cup of rice
- 1 and a half cups of water
- Extra virgin olive oil
- Salt
- Ground pepper
- 1 bay leaf

Instructions

1. We place the clams in salt water so that they are cleaned of sand. We wash well.
2. Chop the onion and the garlic cloves.
3. We put in a pan a little extra virgin olive oil.
4. Fry the onion and garlic cloves.
5. When the onion is transparent, add the clean and chopped tagarninas. We jump well.
6. Season with salt and pepper and go to the Crock Pot.
7. Add the rice and mix well so that the rice mixes well with the sauce.
8. Drain the clams and add them to the Crock Pot.
9. We incorporate the water or broth with the bay leaf.
10. Cover the Crock Pot and cook for 2 hours over high heat.
11. We check that the rice is tender, if not, we will leave more time, it will depend a lot on the rice we have used.
12. We rectify the salt. We serve.

Chickpeas with spinach

For: 4 people

Ingredients

- 300 g of chickpeas + 200 g of spinach
- 1 head of garlic
- 1 teaspoon sweet paprika
- 1 teaspoon ground cumin
- 1 slice of bread
- Extra virgin olive oil + Salt
- 1 bay leaf

Instructions

1. We put the chickpeas to soak for 12 hours minimum. I put them on last night.
2. Once we have soaked the chickpeas, drain them and put them in the Crock Pot.
3. Cover them with water, add a drizzle of extra virgin olive oil, salt and bay leaf.
4. We program the pot for 12 hours at high temperature and let it cook without lifting the lid at any time. It is very important not to lift the lid so that the chickpeas do not lose their temperature so that they do not become hard.
5. Peel the garlic and put them in a large pan with a little extra virgin olive oil.
6. When they pick up the colored garlic, add the bread and fry it on both sides.
7. Then, when the bread is fried and the garlic too, add the paprika and cumin. We remove and remove from the fire. You don't leave a lot of time in the fire that burns the paprika.
8. We put everything in the glass of the blender and crush it with a little broth for cooking the chickpeas.
9. If the chickpeas have a lot of water or broth, we remove it so that it does not have as much.
10. Add to the Crock Pot where we have the chickpeas the chopped spinach.
11. Season with salt and pepper and add what we have in the crushed mixing glass.
12. Mix thoroughly and leave for 1 hour more at low temperature.
13. We serve.

Melva with red peppers

For: 4 people

Ingredients

- 1 melva
- 2 onions
- 1 or 2 red peppers
- Extra virgin olive oil
- Salt
- Ground pepper
- Oregano
- Fine wine

Instructions

1. Cut the onion into julienne strips and the peppers into strips.
2. We put the vegetables in a pan with a background of extra virgin olive oil and cook over low heat.
3. Peel the garlic and add it chopped or rolled.
4. When the onion is transparent, add it to the bowl of the Crock Pot.
5. We cut the melva into four pieces.
6. We place the melva on the onion and peppers.
7. Season with salt and pepper and add a little oregano.
8. We incorporate a little good wine.
9. Cover the Crock Pot and select high heat, 1 hour.
10. We serve.

Pork leg with sauce and red peppers

For 4 people

Ingredients

- Pork leg on a slice
- 1 large onion
- 1 tomato
- 1 roasted red pepper
- 4 garlic cloves
- Extra virgin olive oil
- Salt
- Ground pepper
- 1 glass of wine

Instructions

1. We put the peeled and chopped vegetables on the bottom of the Crock Pot.
2. On the vegetables we place the piece of meat, season and add a little extra virgin olive oil and wine.
3. We cover the Crock Pot.
4. We select 7 hours, low temperature.
5. At the end of the program, we take the piece of meat to a tray so that it loses some heat.
6. All vegetables with broth we pour into a saucepan.
7. We set the fire to reduce.
8. Crush to obtain the red pepper sauce with which we will serve the meat.
9. We rectify the salt.
10. We cut the piece of pork leg into fillets.
11. We serve with the sauce.

Veal rolls

For: 4 people

Ingredients

- 4 large and fine veal tenderloins or 8 medium
- Slices of cheese
- Slices of raw or cooked ham
- Extra virgin olive oil
- Came
- 1 onion
- 1 roasted red pepper
- Salt
- Ground pepper
- Potato chips to accompany

Instructions

1. We lay out the beef fillets and season with salt and pepper.
2. We place a slice of cheese and another of ham.
3. Roll up and put inside the Crock Pot.
4. Cut the onion and pepper into strips and put in a pan with a little extra virgin olive oil.
5. We make the sofrito over low heat.
6. Season with salt and pepper and add the wine.
7. We are boiling.
8. We pass the sofrito to the Crock Pot, on top of the beef rolls.
9. We select high cooking 6 hours.
10. We serve with fried potatoes.

Chicken breast with peppers

For: 4 people

Ingredients

- 4 small chicken breasts
- 1 red pepper
- 1 onion
- 50g extra virgin olive oil
- Salt
- Ground pepper
- 30g of wine
- 1 bay leaf
- Green beans sautéed with a little garlic to accompany

Instructions

1. Season the breasts with salt and pepper and put them in the Crock Pot.
2. Chop the onion and the red pepper. We put it in a pan with the oil and make the sauce. I made it on the Thermomix. Just add the onion and red pepper and select 5 seconds speed 5. Add the oil and select 7 minutes, 120 degrees temperature, speed 1.
3. We put the sofrito on the chicken breasts.
4. Add wine and bay leaf.
5. We cover the Crock Pot and leave in less than 6 hours.
6. We check that the breasts are well cooked, it will depend on their size that we must have them longer.
7. We remove the breasts and cut them into fillets.
8. The sauce can be reduced a little on the fire, it can be crushed or left as it is.
9. We serve the meat with sautéed green beans and the sauce.

Chickpeas with Swiss chard

For 4 people

Ingredients

- 1 jar of cooked chickpeas
- 1 pot of cooked Swiss chard
- 6 garlic cloves
- 1 slice of bread, diced
- 1 teaspoon paprika
- Extra virgin olive oil
- Salt

Instructions

1. Drain the Swiss chard.
2. Add extra virgin olive oil to a pan.
3. Add bread and garlic cloves.
4. Fry and when ready, turn off the heat, add the paprika and stir.
5. Crush the bread with the garlic cloves, oil and paprika in the mortar. You can also crush with the blender.
6. We put the chickpeas with the Swiss chard in the Crock Pot. We blend.
7. Add the puree, mix well.
8. We add a small glass of water, it does not have to cover.
9. We put salt to taste.
10. We select the high cooking and leave 1 hour of cooking.
11. We serve.

Veal Broth

For 4 people

Ingredients

- ½ chicken
- 200g beef bones
- 300g beef brisket
- 1 chicken carcass
- 1 slice of ham bone
- 1 leek
- 1 carrot
- 1 turnip
- 2 stalks of celery
- 1 sprig of peppermint
- Water

Instructions

1. We put in the Crock Pot the chicken, the veal and ham bones, the veal and the chicken carcass.
2. On the meats, we put the well-washed white part of the leek, the peeled and chopped carrot, the peeled turnip and the celery without the leaves, chopped.
3. We cover with water.
4. Cover and select high doneness.
5. We let it cook for 12 hours.
6. Add the peppermint and let stand for 20 minutes.
7. We remove the vegetables and we remove the meats with the bones.
8. We strain the broth with a cloth strainer.
9. We already have the broth to serve as we want, I put the broth in a saucepan, on the fire and added 300 gr of small stars. Cook until tender.
10. You can add to the broth, the chopped carrot and the celery, if you want
11. We serve.

Pork leg in red wine

For 4 people

Ingredients

- 1 piece of pork thigh
- 1 onion
- 1 tomato
- 1 bell pepper
- 4 garlic cloves
- Extra virgin olive oil
- Salt
- Ground pepper
- 1 glass of red wine

Instructions

1. We put everything in the Crock Pot. The peeled and chopped vegetables at the bottom, on top we place the piece of meat, salt and pepper and add a little extra virgin olive oil and red wine.
2. We cover the Crock Pot.
3. We select 7 hours, low temperature.
4. We let it cook for these hours and when it ends, we take out the piece of meat and put it on a tray so that it loses a little heat.
5. Any contents that remained in the Crock Pot are transferred to a saucepan and brought to a fire to reduce the liquids.
6. We crush to obtain the sauce with which we will serve the meat.
7. If we still feel it very liquid, we put another time on the fire so that it evaporates and decreases.
8. We cut the meat into fillets.
9. We serve the meat with the sauce.

Rosemary Pork Chops

For: 4 people

Ingredients

- 1 pork chop
- Extra virgin olive oil
- Salt
- Ground pepper
- Rosemary

Instructions

1. Season the pork chops and cut them into pieces or strips.
2. We put the ribs in the bowl of the Crock Pot.
3. We add extra virgin olive oil.
4. Add a little water, like half a glass. If you want, instead of water, we can put a little beer or wine.
5. On the ribs we put rosemary.
6. We cover the Crock Pot and select the LOW position and leave 6 o'clock.
7. We serve.
8. NOTE: if we want the juices from the Crock Pot as a sauce, we go to a saucepan and turn on the heat until it decreases.

Veal churrascos

For: 4 people

Ingredients

- 8 beef churrascos
- Extra virgin olive oil
- Salt
- Ground pepper
- A few sprigs of fresh rosemary
- 4 garlic cloves

Instructions

1. We put in the bowl of the Crock For the peeled and whole garlic cloves.
2. Add a little extra virgin olive oil.
3. Add the previously seasoned beef churrascos.
4. We put the sprigs of rosemary.
5. Cover and leave on high for about 4 hours or on low for about 8 hours, as desired.
6. Once the churrascos are cooked, put a little oil in a pan and heat well.
7. We mark the steaks on both sides until browned.
8. We serve.

Chicken thighs

For 4 people

Ingredients

- 8 skinless chicken thighs
- 1 onion
- 1 green pepper
- 1 carrot
- 4 garlic cloves
- 50g extra virgin olive oil
- Salt
- Ground pepper
- 1 bay leaf
- 1 glass of wine

Instructions

1. We put the vegetables in the Thermomix and select the speed 5 seconds 5.
2. We go down the walls and add the oil.
3. We select 7 minutes, 120 degrees temperature, speed 1.
4. We pass the sofrito which leads to the bottom of the Crock Pot.
5. On the sofrito we put the thighs without skin.
6. Season with salt and pepper and add the bay leaf.
7. We put a little water, like half a glass.
8. We add wine .
9. We let it cook at low temperature, we leave it for 5 hours.
10. We serve with fries.
11. If we want the thick sauce, we put the sauce in a saucepan and bring to the fire until it is thick to our liking.

Chicken cooked in beer

For: 4 people

Ingredients

- 1 ground chicken
- Salt
- Ground pepper
- garlic powder
- onion powder
- Extra virgin olive oil
- 1 can of beer

Instructions

1. We put the chicken in the bowl of the Crock Pot.
2. Season the chicken.
3. Sprinkle with garlic and onion powder.
4. Add the thyme.
5. We put a few threads of extra virgin olive oil.
6. We add the can of beer.
7. We take the Crock Pot, high done, 4 hours.
8. We transfer the chicken to a dish and set aside.
9. All the sauce that has the Crock Pot bucket we put in a saucepan and take to the fire.
10. We let the sauce reduce until it thickens to our liking.
11. Add the sauce to the chicken.
12. We serve.

Chicken thighs with beans

For 4 people

Ingredients

- 8 chicken thighs
- 1 onion
- 1 pot of vegetable stew
- Extra virgin olive oil
- Salt
- Ground pepper
- 1 glass of wine

Instructions

1. In a pan we put the chopped onion and a little extra virgin olive oil.
2. When the onion is transparent, add the thighs and brown on all sides.
3. Season with salt and pepper, add the wine and bring to a boil.
4. We go to the Crock Pot.
5. We select low temperature and leave for 4 hours.
6. After this time, drain the stew and add it to the Crock Pot.
7. Mix thoroughly and leave for about 20 minutes more.
8. We rectify the salt.
9. We serve.

Chicken steaks with vegetables

For 4 people

Ingredients

- 8 chicken churrascos
- 2 or carrots
- 1 onion
- 4 garlic cloves
- 1 zucchini
- 1 eggplant
- Extra virgin olive oil
- 1 glass of good wine
- Salt
- Ground pepper

Instructions

1. Add a drizzle of extra virgin olive oil to a pan.
2. We brown the steaks on both sides. I removed the skin but you can leave it on if you want more.
3. Seasoned and put in the Crock Pot.
4. To this oil, if necessary, add a little more and add the onion cut into julienne strips and the rolled garlic.
5. We cut the carrot, eggplant and zucchini.
6. We add it to the pan and sauté.
7. We put the wine and boil it.
8. We pass all this vegetable, which is only lightly sautéed but not finished cooking, to the Crock Pot.
9. Cover the Crock Pot and leave on high for 3 hours.
10. We rectify the salt.
11. We serve.

Chickpea menudo

For: 4-8

Ingredients

- 1 kg and a half often
- 300 grams of chickpeas
- 2 fresh chorizo
- 1 blood sausage
- 1 head of garlic
- 1 piece of ham
- 2 bay leaves
- 1 onion
- 10 cloves
- 10 whole bell peppers
- 1 teaspoon hot paprika
- Salt
- Cayenne to taste

Instructions

1. In a saucepan or saucepan, bring the small pieces to a boil to foam and blanch them. Do not skip this step, you must often clean well. Let boil for about 30 minutes. Drain, wash well under running water and drain well.
2. We often put it in the bowl of the Crock Pot.
3. We incorporate the chickpeas that we had to soak all night, drained from the water where they soaked.
4. Peel the onion and add it whole.
5. We leave the garlic whole and add it to the bucket.
6. We put bay leaf, cayenne, cloves, peppers, salt to taste and paprika.
7. We cut the ham into cubes, cut the chorizo and the blood sausage into cubes as well. We add everything.
8. Remove to mix the ingredients.
9. We cover with very hot water. Just cover because as it does not boil, the broth barely evaporates.

10. Cover the Crock Pot and select HIGH, 12 hours.

11. Onion and head of garlic are discarded.

12. We rectify the salt if necessary.

13. We serve.

Multi-meat dish

For: 4 people

Ingredients

- 1 leek + 1 turnip
- 1 stalk of celery
- 1 potato + 1 carrot
- 150g chickpeas
- 1 white bone + 1 prickly
- 1 piece of salt rib
- 1 piece of salted bacon
- 1 drumstick chicken thigh
- 1 piece of veal shank
- 1 chicken shell (optional)

Instructions

1. We put the chickpeas to soak for at least 6 hours.
2. Drain the chickpeas and put them in the Crock Pot.
3. We continue to add the peeled and chopped vegetables, the potato and the carrot, the apiom the leek and the turnip.
4. We wash the bones to remove excess salt. We incorporate them with the bacon and the meats.
5. Cover with water and cover.
6. We select high or high temperature cooking and leave for 8 hours.
7. When ready, remove the bones and discard.
8. We move the chicken, beef and bacon to a tray, this will be our second course.
9. The first course is the chickpea and vegetable broth or the broth in which you can put a little angel hair noodles which in a few minutes boiling in the broth, they can be tender.
10. The broth should be strained to remove excess fat.
11. We serve the noodles first and the meat with the bacon as the second course.

Pork head loin

For: 4 people

Ingredients

- 1 pig's head
- Salt
- Ground pepper
- Thyme
- Extra virgin olive oil
- 20ml wine
- 1 onion
- 4 garlic cloves

Instructions

1. Season the pork head and sprinkle with thyme.
2. In a large pan, put a little extra virgin olive oil.
3. We seal the pig's head on all its faces.
4. We go to the bowl of the Crock Pot.
5. We add a little extra virgin olive oil to the pan.
6. Add the chopped onion and make the sauce.
7. When the onion is transparent, add the wine and bring to a boil.
8. We pass the onion with all the liquid we have in the pan in the bowl of the Crock Pot over the meat.
9. Select the slow position and leave for 6 hours.
10. Remove the piece of pig's head and set aside.
11. Once cold, you can cut.
12. We can mash the onion with a little juice to make a rich sauce to accompany pork tenderloin steaks.

Calf at the planter

For: 4 people

Ingredients

- 700 grams of beef black pudding
- 2 carrots
- 1 onion
- 1 green pepper
- 1 red pepper
- 2 cloves garlic
- 100ml white wine
- Plain flour
- 50ml extra virgin olive oil
- 1 bay leaf
- Ground pepper
- Salt

Instructions

1. Chop the onion, green pepper, red pepper and garlic.
2. Peel the carrots and cut them into half moons or squares.
3. We put in a frying pan half the oil and add the vegetables.
4. Fry the vegetables a little, about 5 minutes and set aside.
5. We cut the veal black pudding and season it with salt and pepper.
6. We pass the meat through the flour and shake it.
7. In the same pan as before, we put the other oil we have and brown the meat when it is hot. Leave to boil for a few minutes so that the alcohol evaporates the wine.
8. We pass the entire contents of the pot to the CrockPot.
9. We add the bay leaf to the meat and cook for 6 hours on low selection.
10. Register our meat at the planter.

Iberian loin

For: 4 people

Ingredients

- 1 kg of Iberian loin tips
- 150 ml water + 50 ml balsamic vinegar
- Salt + ground pepper
- Thyme + Extra virgin olive oil
- 20ml wine
- 1 onion
- 4 garlic cloves

Instructions

1. Season the Iberian loin tips with salt and pepper.
2. Sprinkle with thyme.
3. In a large pan, put a little extra virgin olive oil.
4. We seal the ends of the Iberian loin on all sides.
5. We go to the bowl of the Crock Pot.
6. We add a little extra virgin olive oil to the pan.
7. Add the chopped onion.
8. We incorporate the peeled and whole garlic cloves.
9. We jump.
10. When the onion is transparent, add the vinegar and water.
11. When it starts to boil, we go into the Crock Pot bucket.
12. Select the slow position and leave for 6 hours.
13. We remove the pieces of the Iberian loin tip and reserve them.
14. We transfer the juice from the bucket to the pan with onion and garlic cloves.
15. Add the wine and simmer until the sauce is slightly reduced.
16. We go to the blender glass and mash.
17. We cut the ends of the Iberian loin into thin fillets.
18. We serve the meat with the sauce.

Potatoes with meat, green beans and carrots

For 4 people

Ingredients

- 500 g of pork
- 300 g of potatoes
- 1 onion
- 2 cloves garlic
- 1 bell pepper
- 1 tomato
- 2 carrots
- 100 g of green beans
- Salt
- Ground pepper
- 1 pinch of sweet paprika
- 1 small glass of water
- 1 small wine
- Extra virgin olive oil

Instructions

1. We put in a frying pan a bottom of extra virgin olive oil.
2. Add the meat and sauté until browned.
3. Season with salt and pepper and add the wine.
4. We bring to a boil and put the meat in the Crock Pot.
5. We select high cooking and coverage.
6. Chop the onion, garlic, bell pepper and tomato.
7. We put everything in the pan from before with a little extra virgin olive oil.
8. We jump.
9. When the onion is transparent, add a pinch of paprika and stir.
10. Add to Crock Pot and stir. with the meat so that everything is mixed.
11. We let it cook for 2 hours at the same temperature as before, high.

12. Peel the potatoes and chop them. Peel the carrots and chop them. We cut the green beans into pieces, removing the tips.
13. We add the potatoes, carrots and green beans to the Crock Pot.
14. Season and mix everything.
15. Add the preheated glass of water to the Crock Pot.
16. We leave high cooking for another two hours.
17. We check that the potato is tender, we rectify with salt and broth if necessary.
18. We serve.

Iberian pork cheek

For: 4 -6 people

Ingredients

- 1 kg of Iberian pork cheek
- 2 onions
- 1 head of garlic
- Extra virgin olive oil
- 1 large glass of wine
- Salt
- Ground pepper

Instructions

1. Chop the cheek previously freed from fat.
2. We season and reserve .
3. Chop the onion and roll the garlic.
4. In a large skillet, put the onion and garlic with a base of extra virgin olive oil.
5. We add the meat.
6. We jump.
7. Add the wine and bring to a boil.
8. Season with salt and pepper.
9. We spent it all at the Crock Pot.
10. Cover and select high doneness.
11. We let it cook for 5 hours.
12. We rectify the salt.
13. We serve.

Chickpeas with Swiss chard

For 4 people

Ingredients

- 300 g of chickpeas
- 1 bunch Swiss chard
- 1 head of garlic
- ½ teaspoon sweet paprika
- 1 onion
- 1 teaspoon ground cumin
- Extra virgin olive oil

Instructions

1. We put the chickpeas to soak for 12 hours minimum.
2. Once we have soaked the chickpeas, drain them and put them in the Crock Pot.
3. Cover them with water so that we have the water above the chickpeas.
4. We program the pot for 12 hours at high temperature and let it cook without lifting the lid at any time. It is very important not to lift the lid so that the chickpeas do not lose temperature.
5. When an hour is missing, chop the garlic and put it in a large skillet or saucepan with a generous drizzle of extra virgin olive oil.
6. When they take color, we add paprika and cumin. We remove from the fire.
7. We add the chopped and washed Swiss chard.
8. We return to the fire and sauté the chard well. Season with salt and pepper.
9. We add to the chickpeas that we can uncover, and bind carefully so as not to break the chickpeas too much.
10. We cover again and let the program complete.
11. Fix salt and serve.

Potatoes with Swiss chard

For 4 people

Ingredients

- 8 medium potatoes
- 1 large Swiss chard
- 4 garlic cloves
- Extra virgin olive oil
- 1 teaspoon paprika
- Salt
- Ground pepper
- Cumin
- To accompany, the filet mignon steaks and the eggs

Instructions

1. Peel the potatoes and chop them.
2. We wash and put in the Crock Pot.
3. Season with salt and pepper.
4. Chop the Swiss chard, wash and add the potatoes.
5. In a frying pan we put a generous amount of oil and we fry the rolled garlic.
6. When they are fried, without too much color, remove from the heat and add the paprika and a little cumin.
7. We remove and add to the Crock Pot.
8. We remove the potatoes and Swiss chard so that the oil and garlic soak everything.
9. Add a pinch of water, very little.
10. Cover the Crock Pot and select high heat, 2 hours.
11. We poke a potato and if it is tender, turn off the Crock Pot.
12. We rectify with salt and serve with fried eggs and grilled loin fillets.

Vegetables with eggs

Makes: 2 servings

Ingredients

- 1 onion
- 1 green pepper
- 1 red pepper
- 1 zucchini
- 1 eggplant
- 4 ripe tomatoes
- 4 eggs
- Extra virgin olive oil
- Salt
- Ground pepper
- garlic powder

Instructions

1. Peel and cut all the vegetables into small cubes.
2. We put the vegetables, well mixed, in the bowl of the Crock Pot.
3. We add a few threads of extra virgin olive oil.
4. Season and sprinkle with garlic powder.
5. Mix and cover the Crock Pot.
6. We select 3 hours, high temperature.
7. We break the eggs over the vegetables and again cover the Crock Pot with the lid.
8. We leave between 10 and 20 minutes more, it will depend on how you like the egg curds.
9. We serve.

Chicken thighs with vegetables

For 4 people

Ingredients

- 8 chicken thighs
- 120 g of green beans
- 2 or 3 carrots
- 1 onion
- 8 garlic cloves
- Extra virgin olive oil
- 1 glass of good wine
- Salt
- Ground pepper

Instructions

1. We put in a frying pan a bottom of extra virgin olive oil.
2. Add the chicken thighs and brown on all sides. I removed the skin so it wasn't seasoned and we went to the Crock Pot.
3. To this oil, if you need a little more, we add it, we add the onion cut into julienne and the rolled garlic.
4. Add the wine when the onion is transparent and bring to a boil.
5. We Crock Pot the onion with the garlic and all the juice from the pan.
6. Cover the Crock Pot and leave on high for 2 hours.
7. Chop carrots and green beans.
8. We add carrots and green beans to the Crock Pot.
9. We cook for another 2 hours at high temperature.
10. We rectify the salt.
11. We serve.

Beef with tomato

For: 4 people

Ingredients

- 1 can of large crushed tomato (500 grams)
- 1 onion
- 4 garlic cloves
- 1 kg of beef
- Extra virgin olive oil
- Salt
- Ground pepper
- 1 small glass of red wine

Instructions

1. We put in a pan the very chopped onion with a bottom of extra virgin olive oil.
2. When the onion is transparent, add the can of tomato.
3. When it begins to boil, season with salt and pepper and strain into the Crock Pot.
4. Leave on low heat for 2 hours.
5. In a pan we put the chopped garlic with a little extra virgin olive oil.
6. Add the diced beef and sauté to brown on all sides.
7. Season with salt and pepper and add the wine.
8. We are boiling.
9. When the tomato has been cooking for two hours, add the veal that we have in the pan and mix well.
10. We leave for haute cuisine, 6 o'clock.
11. We rectify the salt.
12. We serve the meat with tomato on fried potatoes.

Turkey breast roll

For: 4 people

Ingredients

- 1 turkey breast
- Salt
- Ground pepper
- Sliced cheese
- Ham
- 1 onion
- 1 green pepper
- 1 red pepper
- Extra virgin olive oil
- 12 mushrooms
- 1 splash of white wine

Instructions

1. We open the turkey breast so that it is as thin as possible.
2. Season with salt and pepper.
3. We put the cheese and raw ham.
4. Roll up, press well and leave in the freezer for a few minutes.
5. In a pan we put a bottom of extra virgin olive oil.
6. Add onion, peppers and mushrooms, all cut into pieces.
7. We make the sofrito over low heat.
8. When the sofrito is ready, we pass it into the bowl of the Crock Pot.
9. On top of the vegetables we put the roll of turkey breast stuffed with ham and cheese.
10. Season with salt and pepper and add a little wine.
11. We select high cooking and leave for 5 hours.
12. We take out the roll and cut it.
13. We put the vegetables in a spring, the sliced roll on top and add the sauce from the bowl of the Crock Pot. We serve.

Chicken with carrots

For 4 people

Ingredients

- 1 chicken
- 120 g of peas
- 2 or 3 carrots
- 1 onion
- 8 garlic cloves
- Extra virgin olive oil
- 1 glass of good wine
- Salt
- Ground pepper

Instructions

1. We put a drizzle of extra virgin olive oil in a pan and add the seasoned chicken pieces, without the skin.
2. We brown a bit and move on to the Crock Pot.
3. In this oil, brown the onion cut in julienne and the rolled garlic.
4. When the onion is fried, we move everything to the Crock Pot.
5. Add the wine to the saucepan, bring to a boil and return to the Crock Pot over the chicken.
6. Cover the Crock Pot and leave on high for 2 hours.
7. Chop the carrots.
8. We add the carrots and peas to the Crock Pot and leave for another 2 hours on high.
9. We rectify the salt.
10. We serve.

Beef with vegetables

For 4 people

Ingredients

- 1 kg diced meat
- 1 onion
- 2 cloves garlic
- 1 bag of frozen stew
- Salt
- Ground pepper
- 1 glass of wine
- Extra virgin olive oil

Instructions

1. Add a base of extra virgin olive oil to the pan.
2. Add the diced meat.
3. We jump and lounge and pepper.
4. Add the wine and bring to a strong boil.
5. Chop the onion and the garlic.
6. Add the onion and garlic to the meat and sauté.
7. When the onion is transparent, we pass everything to the Crock Pot.
8. We select haute cuisine.
9. We let it cook for 2 hours.
10. Add the stew to the Crock Pot and stir. If we see that it does not have a lot of broth, we put a little hot water or hot broth.
11. We leave high cooking for another 2 hours.
12. We check that the vegetables are tender.
13. We rectify the salt.
14. We serve.

Chicken breasts

For 4 people

Ingredients

- 2 chicken breasts
- 1 lemon
- Salt
- Ground pepper
- Extra virgin olive oil
- garlic powder
- Thyme

Instructions

1. We put both breasts in a bowl and season on both sides.
2. Add garlic powder and sprinkle with thyme.
3. Squeeze the lemon and add it to the bowl where we have the chicken breasts.
4. Leave to marinate for about 15 minutes.
5. We put the breasts in the Crock Pot with all the juice from the bowl.
6. We incorporate a few threads of extra virgin olive oil.
7. We select a high temperature and leave for about 3 hours.
8. We transfer the breasts to the cutting board and put all the juice in a saucepan to reduce the sauce.
9. We cut the breasts into fillets and serve with the reduced sauce.

Pork loin with bun

Makes: 12 servings

Ingredients

- 1 whole pork loin
- 12 garlic cloves
- 1 onion
- Extra virgin olive oil
- Salt
- Ground pepper
- 1 glass of whiskey
- 12 buns

Instructions

1. We put in a pan a little extra virgin olive oil.
2. Add the garlic, peeled and chopped.
3. Add chopped onion.
4. When the garlic cloves begin to turn soft and the onion transparent, add the previously seasoned piece of pork loin.
5. We gild for all their faces.
6. Add the whiskey to the meat and bring to a strong boil.
7. We pass the entire contents of the pan to the Crock Pot.
8. Season with salt and pepper.
9. Select low heat and cook with the Crock Pot covered for 6 hours.
10. Let the meat cool completely inside the Crock Pot.
11. Transfer the onion and garlic cloves to the blender glass with some of the juice and mash.
12. We cut the pork loin with the cold strawberry.
13. We open the loaves and distribute the meat between them. Serve with the sauce.

Pork loin with herbs, thyme and rosemary

For 4 people
Ingredients
- 1 pork loin
- 150ml water
- 50ml balsamic vinegar
- Salt
- Ground pepper
- Rosemary
- Thyme
- Extra virgin olive oil
- 1 tablespoon of flour
- 20ml wine
- 1 onion
- 4 garlic cloves

Instructions
1. Season the pork loin with salt and pepper and sprinkle with thyme and rosemary.
2. In a large pan, put a little extra virgin olive oil.
3. We seal the pork loin on all sides.
4. We go to the bowl of the Crock Pot.
5. We add a little extra virgin olive oil to the pan.
6. Add the chopped onion and the peeled and whole garlic cloves.
7. We make the sofrito.
8. When the onion is transparent, add the vinegar and water.
9. When it starts boiling, we pass the Crock Pot over the meat.
10. Select the slow position and leave for 6 hours.
11. We remove the piece of loin and set aside.
12. We transfer the juice from the bucket to the pan with onion and garlic cloves.

13. Add the wine and bring to a simmer, stirring.

14. We dilute a tablespoon of flour in a little cold water.

15. When we have the flour well bound, we move on to the pan.

16. We bind well and crush everything with the blender to obtain a thin sauce.

17. We cut the piece of pork loin into thin fillets.

18. We serve the meat with the sauce.

Veal chop with potatoes and paprika

For 4 people

Ingredients

- 500 g beef ribs
- 800 g of potatoes
- 1 onion
- 4 garlic cloves
- 1 glass of white wine
- Extra virgin olive oil
- Salt
- Ground pepper
- 1 teaspoon sweet paprika

Instructions

1. Add a base of extra virgin olive oil to a large frying pan.
2. Add the beef ribs.
3. Chop the onion and garlic, all very fine.
4. We add everything to the pan.
5. Sauté and let the ribs seal and the onion becomes tender.
6. Season with salt and pepper.
7. Add paprika and stir.
8. Add the wine and bring to a strong boil.
9. We pass everything we have in the pan into the bowl of the Crock Pot.
10. We select haute cuisine.
11. Peel the potatoes and chop them.
12. Add to Crock Pot and mix well so that all ingredients are combined.
13. We add a little water. just enough for the potatoes to cook.
14. We cover, go HIGH, 4 o'clock. To serve.

Potatoes with ribs

For 4 people

Ingredients

- 500 g ribs
- 800 g of potatoes
- 1 onion
- 1 green pepper
- 1 red pepper
- 1 glass of white wine
- Extra virgin olive oil
- Salt
- Ground pepper
- 1 bay leaf

Instructions

1. We put in a large frying pan a bottom of extra virgin olive oil.
2. Add the ribs.
3. Chop the onion and add it.
4. We skip everything well so that the ribs are sealed.
5. Chop the two peppers and add them.
6. When we see the vegetables tender, we add the wine.
7. We bring it to a boil and transfer everything to the Crock Pot.
8. Peel the potatoes and chop them.
9. Add and mix well to combine everything.
10. Season with salt and pepper, add the bay leaf and add a little water.
11. We put the Crock Pot on high heat, 4 hours.
12. Fix salt and serve.

Pork Loin with Worcestershire Sauce

For 4 people

Ingredients

- 1 pork loin + 1 onion
- 4 garlic cloves
- 2 tablespoons Worcestershire sauce
- 1 teaspoon garlic powder
- 1 teaspoon sweet paprika
- Ground pepper
- Salt + Extra virgin olive oil

Instructions

1. We season the pork loin on all sides.
2. In a large pan, put a drizzle of extra virgin olive oil and brown the loin on all sides.
3. We reserve.
4. Chop the onion and the garlic.
5. In the pan before putting a little oil and adding the onion and garlic.
6. We start making the sofrito.
7. When the onion is transparent, add the Worcestershire sauce, garlic powder and paprika.
8. Remove from the heat and stir in circles with the pan.
9. We put the loin in the Crock Pot and add on top of all the contents of the pan.
10. Select low heat and cook for 6-8 hours depending on the thickness of the loin and how we like the meat cooked inside.
11. We remove the loin and when it is completely cold, we cut it into the cold strawberry.
12. The onion and garlic sauce that we left in the pot is crushed with the blender so that there is a thin sauce.
13. We serve the meat with the hot sauce on top.

Potatoes with beef

For: 4 people

Ingredients

- 500 grams of beef
- 800 grams of potatoes
- 1 onion
- 2 cloves garlic
- 1 bell pepper
- 1 tomato
- Salt
- Ground pepper
- 1 glass of water
- 1 glass of red wine
- Extra virgin olive oil

Instructions

1. We put in a frying pan a bottom of extra virgin olive oil.
2. We add the beef.
3. We brown and we season
4. We incorporate the wine into the red wine.
5. We bring a strong boil,
6. We add the beef to the Crock Pot with all the juices.
7. We select high cooking and coverage.
8. In the same pan, add a little extra virgin olive oil.
9. Chop the onion, garlic, bell pepper and tomato.
10. Add to the skillet and make the sauce.
11. When the onion is transparent, add to the Crock Pot and stir.
12. We let it cook for 4 hours in the high position.
13. Peel the potatoes and chop them. We wash and reserve.
14. When time passes, we add the potatoes to the Crock Pot.
15. We put the glass of water, very hot so that it does not change the temperature of the beef stew.

16. We leave the upper kitchen for another two hours.

17. We check that the potatoes are well cooked.

18. We rectify the salt and broth if necessary.

19. We serve.

Pork meat with Pedro Jiménez

For: 6 -8 people

Ingredients

- 1 piece of pork leg
- 3 onions
- 6 garlic cloves
- Extra virgin olive oil
- Pedro Jimenez
- Salt
- Ground pepper

Instructions

1. We put in a frying pan or a large saucepan a bottom of extra virgin olive oil and add the onion cut in julienne and the whole garlic.
2. We let the sauce be made.
3. We pass the sofrito at the bottom of the Crock Pot.
4. In the same container, brown the piece of meat.
5. We place the meat on the sofrito.
6. In the same container we put a few glasses of Pedro Jiménez and when it starts to boil, add the meat to the top.
7. Season with salt and pepper.
8. Cover the Crock Pot and select low cook.
9. We let it cook for 6 hours.
10. We turn the piece of meat over and leave to cook for another 4 hours.
11. In order for the meat to cut well without breaking, we must have the piece of meat cold.
12. All the onions and garlic are crushed in a blender and you get a rich sauce to serve with the meat. We serve the sauce very hot.

Whiskey sirloin

For 4 people

Ingredients

- 2 large sirloin
- 12 garlic cloves
- 1 onion
- Extra virgin olive oil
- Salt
- Ground pepper
- 1 glass of whiskey

Instructions

1. Add a drizzle of extra virgin olive oil to a pan.
2. Add the peeled and whole garlic.
3. Add chopped onion.
4. When the garlic cloves begin to turn soft and the onion transparent, add the two whole sirloins.
5. We brown the sirloins all over their faces.
6. Add the whiskey to the saucepan and bring to a strong boil.
7. We put garlic and onion on the bottom of the slow cooker.
8. On top we put the two sirloins.
9. Season with salt and pepper.
10. We select high temperature and leave, covered, 3 hours.
11. We let the fillets cool inside the Crock Pot.
12. We take out the sirloins.
13. Transfer the onion and garlic cloves to the blender glass. We crush.
14. We cut the fillets into medallions.
15. We serve with the sauce.

Lentils with green beans and carrots

For 4 people

Ingredients

- 300g brown lentils
- 1 onion
- 1 bell pepper
- 1 head of garlic
- 1 tomato
- 50g extra virgin olive oil
- 1 teaspoon sweet paprika
- 1 carrot
- 1 potato
- 12 flat green bean pods
- 1 bay leaf
- Salt

Instructions

1. We put the lentils in the Crock Pot.
2. Peel the potato and carrot and cut them into small cubes.
3. Add to lentils. Chop the green beans and add them to the Crock Pot.
4. We blend. Add the whole tomato, the whole pepper, the peeled and whole onion and the head of garlic.
5. Add salt, paprika and bay leaf. Add oil and cover with water.
6. We stir so that all the ingredients are mixed.
7. We cover the Crock Pot.
8. We select at low temperature and cook for 6 to 7 hours.
9. Put the tomato, onion and pepper in the blender glass.
10. We mash the vegetables and pour them into the lentils.
11. Stir to combine well, being careful not to break the lentils too much.
12. We rectify the salt. We serve.

Sausages in wine

For: 4 people

Ingredients

- 12 fresh chicken sausages
- 1 onion
- 3 cloves of garlic
- 50ml white wine
- 100ml extra virgin olive oil
- Salt
- Ground pepper

Instructions

1. We put the oil in the Crock Pot. We select high cooking and coverage.
2. Cut the onion into julienne strips and roll the garlic.
3. We add them to the Crock Pot and stir so that the oil permeates the onion and garlic well.
4. Sauté the sausages in a skillet until they brown slightly on the outside.
5. We place the sausages on the onion.
6. Add the wine and season with salt and pepper.
7. We left to cook, covered the Crock Pot and on high cooking, 3 hours.
8. We serve.

Roasted peppers with mozzarella balls

For 4 people

Ingredients

- 3 large red peppers
- Extra virgin olive oil
- 1 spoon of mozzarella balls
- 6 garlic cloves
- Salt
- Extra virgin olive oil
- Winemaker Sherry

Instructions

1. We put in the bottom of the Crock Pot a little extra virgin olive oil.
2. Add the peeled and whole garlic cloves.
3. We paint the red peppers with extra virgin olive oil.
4. We put them inside the Crock Pot.
5. We leave for 4 hours in haute cuisine.
6. Once the cooking is finished, we let them cool inside and without revealing.
7. After this time, we remove the peppers and remove the skin, peduncle, roasted garlic and seeds.
8. Reserve some of the cooking liquid.
9. We cut the peppers into strips.
10. We prepare a vinaigrette with oil, salt, vinegar and a little of the cooking liquid.
11. Add the vinaigrette to the peppers.
12. Add the well-drained mozzarella balls.
13. We mix everything well.
14. Serve, if desired, sprinkled with a little oregano.

Chicken with mushrooms and rice

For: 4 people

Ingredients

- 1 large chicken breast
- 1 bag of assorted mushrooms
- 1 onion
- 2 cloves garlic
- Extra virgin olive oil
- 1 small glass of wine
- 200 g of rice
- Salt
- Ground pepper

Instructions

1. We put in a pan a little extra virgin olive oil and add the onion cut in julienne and the rolled garlic.
2. When the onion is transparent, we pass the sofrito to the Crock Pot.
3. In the same skillet we diced the chicken breast, seasoned and sautéed, just a little and poured into the Crock Pot.
4. We put the wine in the pan and bring it to a boil.
5. We pass the wine to the Crock Pot.
6. Add a little salt, ground pepper and add the pre-thawed assorted mushrooms.
7. We link and cover.
8. We select high temperature and cook for 1 hour. It will depend on the size of our chicken.
9. We serve with a little rice previously cooked in water with a little salt.

Loin stuffed with cheddar and ham

For 4 people

Ingredients

- 1 pork loin
- Slices of cooked ham
- Slices of cheddar cheese
- Extra virgin olive oil
- Salt + ground pepper
- 1 onion + 4 garlic cloves
- 1 glass of wine

Instructions

1. We cut the loin as if it were fillets, but without finishing.
2. In each cut we put a slice of cheddar cheese and a slice of cooked ham.
3. We are pressing hard to close.
4. Season with salt and pepper.
5. Place the stuffed loin in the bowl of the Crock Pot.
6. We put the onion and the cloves of garlic, chopped, with a bottom of extra virgin olive oil in a pan.
7. We jump.
8. When the onion is tender, season with salt and pepper and add the wine.
9. We bring to a boil and pass it all through the Crock Pot over the loin.
10. Cover and select slow cook.
11. We let it cook for 12 hours.
12. We take out the loin.
13. We pass the vegetables in the glass of the blender and crush them. Do not put all the liquid, we add according to how we want the liquid or the thick sauce.
14. We serve the fillet with the sauce.

Cauliflower soup

For: 4 people

Ingredients

- 200 g of cauliflower
- 1 leek
- 2 carrots
- 1 large potato
- Extra virgin olive oil
- Salt
- Ground pepper
- 500ml water
- 2 eggs
- 1 piece of semi-cured cheese
- Salt and pepper pistachios

Instructions

1. We put in a large pan the extra virgin olive oil with the leek, carrots and
2. the potato.
3. We fry for 5 minutes.
4. We go to the Crock Pot and add the water, if it is already hot.
5. We select a high function.
6. Chop cauliflower and add to Crock Pot.
7. Season with salt and pepper to taste.
8. We cook 12 hours.
9. We cook the eggs, peel them and chop them.
10. We cut the cheese into small cubes.
11. We peel the pistachios.
12. We serve the soup with cheese, egg and pistachios.

Chicken hindquarter with thyme

Gives: 2

Ingredients

- 2 posteriors
- Salt
- Ground pepper
- dried thyme
- 1 can of beer

Instructions

1. We put the chicken in the Crock Pot, in this case two posteriors.
2. Season with salt and pepper and sprinkle with thyme.
3. We add beer.
4. Cover and select slow cook.
5. We let it cook for 6 hours.
6. We take the hindquarters on a baking sheet with the skin turned up.
7. We cover with all the sauce from the Crock Pot.
8. We take in the oven, at 180 degrees, about 20 minutes or until we see the skin of the chicken golden brown.
9. We serve.

Beef spaghetti

For 4 people

Ingredients

- 2 large beef steaks
- 1 onion
- 2 tomatoes
- 1 roasted green pepper
- 2 carrots
- 1 zucchini
- Extra virgin olive oil
- Salt
- Ground pepper
- 1 glass of red wine
- 300 g of spaghetti

Instructions

1. We put a bottom of oil in a pan and add the chopped onion.
2. When the sauté begins, add the diced tomatoes, bell pepper, half-moon carrots and zucchini.
3. We jump well and go to the Crock Pot.
4. We cut the fillets into strips and add them to the pan.
5. Sauté, season with salt and pepper and add the wine.
6. When it starts boiling, we turn to the Crock Pot.
7. Mix and cover.
8. We select slow cooking and leave for 5 hours.
9. When ready to eat, cook the spaghetti with water and salt.
10. Drain when tender.
11. We go to the Crock Pot and mix.
12. We serve.

Pork loin with zucchini

For 4 people

Ingredients

- 1 piece of pork loin
- 1 onion
- 2 tomatoes
- 1 large pepper
- 1 piece of zucchini
- 4 garlic cloves
- 1 glass of wine
- 1 glass of water If you don't want to put it, nothing happens, everything will be drier but the sauce will be just as delicious
- Extra virgin olive oil
- Salt
- Ground pepper

Instructions

1. We put some extra virgin olive oil in the Crock Pot.
2. Add the loin and chopped vegetables.
3. Season with salt and pepper and add wine and water if desired.
4. We cover.
5. We select slow cooking 7 hours.
6. We remove the loin and cut it into fillets.
7. We mash the vegetables with a little broth, not everything.
8. We serve the meat with the crushed sauce.

Beef steak with mushrooms

For: 4 people

Ingredients

- 800 gr of veal churrascos
- Extra virgin olive oil
- 120 g of mushrooms
- Salt
- 1 teaspoon garlic powder
- 1 teaspoon of pink pepper
- 2 sprigs of fresh rosemary
- 1 small glass of red wine

Instructions

1. In a pan with a little extra virgin olive oil, we will sauté the mushrooms first and then the steaks, so that they are sealed on both sides.
2. We put the mushrooms in the bottom of the Crock Pot and the beef steaks on top.
3. In the pan that we browned the churrascos, add the wine and bring to a boil.
4. The wine with the juices from the pan, we add them to the Crock Pot on the steaks.
5. Season with pink pepper and put the sprigs of rosemary on top.
6. Cover and select slow cook, 7 hours.
7. When serving, you can put a little salt flakes on the churrascos.
8. If we want to serve the juices in sauce, we can go to a saucepan and reduce to high heat until it has the desired texture. Being churrascos, the gelatin from the bones will give us a gelatinous sauce by reducing it over high heat.

Pork stew with vegetables

For: 4 people

Ingredients

- 1 pork tenderloin
- Extra virgin olive oil
- Salt
- Ground pepper
- 1 onion
- 3 cloves of garlic
- 3 medium potatoes
- 100 g of green beans
- 1 carrot
- 1 small broccoli

Instructions

1. In a pan we put the onion cut into julienne strips, the rolled garlic and a drizzle of extra virgin olive oil.
2. We start frying and when we have the transparent onion, we incorporate the sirloin medallions and seal them on both sides.
3. We pass the stir-fry with the sirloin medallions in the bowl of the Crock Pot.
4. We mix well.
5. Peel potatoes and carrot, chop and add to Crock Pot.
6. Chop the green beans and add them too.
7. We cut the broccoli into small sprigs and include them.
8. Season with salt and pepper and add a small glass of water.
9. We cover the Crock Pot and cook on low cook setting, 5 hours.
10. Uncover, adjust the salt and switch to high cooking. We leave another 2 hours. If we see you have a lot of broth, we uncover it to evaporate.
11. We serve.

Printed in Great Britain
by Amazon

27350611R00046